MARTIN LUTHER KING JR. DAY

JILL FORAN

MEDIA ENHANCED BOOKS
AV²
BY WEIGL
ADDED VALUE • AUDIO VISUAL

www.av2books.com

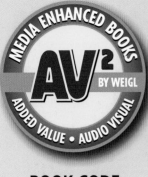

MEDIA ENHANCED BOOKS
AV² BY WEIGL
ADDED VALUE • AUDIO VISUAL

BOOK CODE

W 8 3 4 3 8 8

AV² by Weigl brings you media enhanced books that support active learning.

AV² provides enriched content that supplements and complements this book. Weigl's AV² books strive to create inspired learning and engage young minds for a total learning experience.

Go to **www.av2books.com**, and enter this book's unique code. You will have access to video, audio, web links, quizzes, a slide show, and activities.

Audio
Listen to sections of the book read aloud.

Video
Watch informative video clips.

Web Link
Find research sites and play interactive games.

Try This!
Complete activities and hands-on experiments.

Due to the dynamic nature of the Internet, some of the URLs and activities provided as part of AV² by Weigl may have changed or ceased to exist. AV² by Weigl accepts no responsibility for any such changes. All media enhanced books are regularly monitored to update addresses and sites in a timely manner. Contact AV² by Weigl at 1-866-649-3445 or av2books@weigl.com with any questions, comments, or feedback.

Published by AV² by Weigl
350 5th Avenue, 59th Floor
New York, NY 10118
Website: www.av2books.com   www.weigl.com

Library of Congress Cataloging-in-Publication Data

Foran, Jill.
 Martin Luther King, Jr. Day / Jill Foran.
   p. cm. -- (American celebrations)
 Originally published: c2004.
 Includes index.
 ISBN 978-1-60596-772-1 (hardcover : alk. paper) -- ISBN 978-1-60596-779-0 (softcover : alk. paper) --
 ISBN 978-1-60596-937-4 (e-book)
 1. Martin Luther King, Jr., Day--Juvenile literature. 2. King, Martin Luther, Jr., 1929-1968--Juvenile literature. I. Title.
 E185.97.K5F67 2011
 394.261--dc22
                              2009050988

Printed in the United States of America in North Mankato, Minnesota
1 2 3 4 5 6 7 8 9 0 14 13 12 11 10

05 2010
WEP264000

Editor Heather C. Hudak   **Design** Terry Paulhus

Every reasonable effort has been made to trace ownership and to obtain permission to reprint copyright material. The publishers would be pleased to have any errors or omissions brought to their attention so that they may be corrected in subsequent printings.

Weigl acknowledges Getty Images as its primary image supplier for this title.

CONTENTS

KING

What is Martin Luther King Jr. Day?

On the third Monday of January, Americans celebrate Martin Luther King Jr. Day. This national holiday honors the life of one of America's greatest leaders, Dr. Martin Luther King Jr. He worked very hard to establish freedom for all people and end **segregation** in the United States. Dr. King believed that everyone deserved fair and equal treatment.

Dr. King believed that people should stand up for their **civil rights**. He knew that the best way to do this was through peaceful **protest**, not violence. Dr. King's powerful speeches brought hope to people all over the world.

JANUARY (THIRD MONDAY)
MARTIN LUTHER KING JR. DAY

FEBRUARY (THIRD MONDAY)
PRESIDENTS' DAY

MARCH 17
ST. PATRICK'S DAY

SUNDAY IN MARCH OR APRIL
EASTER

MAY (LAST MONDAY)
MEMORIAL DAY

JUNE 14
FLAG DAY

JULY 4
INDEPENDENCE DAY

AUGUST (FIRST SUNDAY)
FAMILY DAY

SEPTEMBER (FIRST MONDAY)
LABOR DAY

OCTOBER (SECOND MONDAY)
COLUMBUS DAY

NOVEMBER 11
VETERANS DAY

DECEMBER 25
CHRISTMAS DAY

Martin Luther King Jr. Day History

Martin Luther King Jr. was born on January 15, 1929. At the time, African Americans were not treated the same as people of European ancestry. Most southern states had laws that **restricted** African Americans from many activities. They were not allowed in certain parks, hotels, or restaurants.

Dr. King became a minister and a doctor of **theology**. He married Coretta Scott, and they moved to Montgomery, Alabama. There, Dr. King became the minister of the Dexter Avenue Baptist Church. He began to work for changes to the way African Americans were treated. He wanted them to have equal rights.

⭐ **Dr. King received hundreds of awards for his work in civil rights. In 1964, he was given the Nobel Peace Prize. At age 35, he was the youngest man to be awarded the prize.**

Dr. King worked hard for freedom and taught people to stand up for their rights. He had millions of followers. Dr. King wrote many books and articles about the **civil rights movement**. He also wrote powerful speeches. Dr. King said people around the world should fight **injustice** with love. His words inspired listeners to keep working for freedom and **equality**.

In 1968, Dr. King went to Memphis, Tennessee, to join a protest supporting garbage workers who were on **strike**. On April 4, 1968, while standing on the balcony outside his motel room, Dr. King was shot and killed. People around the world were shocked and saddened. Many Americans wanted to honor Dr. King after his death. A holiday for Dr. King was first requested four days after he died.

Past and Present Celebrations

IN 1994 Congress created the King Day of Service to go along with Martin Luther King Jr. Day. The King Day of Service is about helping others and working to fix problems in society. In 2009, people across the United States took part in more than 130,000 volunteer projects.

PRESIDENT REAGAN declared Martin Luther King Jr. Day "a time for rejoicing and reflecting." Today, Martin Luther King Jr. Day is also a time for action. All over the United States, people help those in need and volunteer their time.

AFRICAN AMERICAN students often were not allowed to attend top universities before the civil rights movement. Today, many African American students attend U.S. colleges and universities. Most of these schools hold ceremonies on Martin Luther King, Jr. Day.

Important People

I n Montgomery, Alabama, African Americans had dealt with **unjust laws** for many years. One law stated that African Americans had to sit at the back of any bus they rode. If the bus became full, they had to give up their seats to white passengers.

On December 1, 1955, an African-American woman named Rosa Parks was arrested after she refused to give up her seat to a person of European ancestry. When other African Americans in Montgomery heard what had happened to Rosa, they went to Dr. King for help. Dr. King and other leaders in the community asked fellow African Americans to stay off the buses until the law was changed.

✫✫ Dr. King's father (shown here) and grandfather were also Baptist ministers. They preached at Ebenezer Baptist Church in Atlanta, Georgia.

African Americans who owned cars offered rides to friends and neighbors, but most walked wherever they needed to go. For more than one year, African Americans stayed off the buses. Finally, the courts changed the bus law.

⭐ **Rosa Parks' actions and the bus boycott led to a court case that was taken to the Supreme Court. By December 1956, the court ordered that segregation on Montgomery buses was unconstitutional. Parks' efforts succeeded in changing the law.**

Over time, more and more people marched for equal rights. Finally, the government of the United States passed new laws giving equal treatment to African Americans.

First-hand Account

"We got to the Washington, D.C., YWCA and met with hundreds of other women. We all walked to the Washington Monument, led by women carrying a YWCA banner. Again, an increasing stream of folks approached the Washington Monument…When we arrived at the Lincoln Memorial, we all settled down to hear musicians, civil rights leaders, and celebrities… After Dr. King spoke, we all left Washington, encouraged to continue to strive for racial equality in all areas of life."

In 1963, Martha Wason of Asheville, North Carolina, took part in the March on Washington with the Young Women's Christian Association (YWCA).

Celebrating Today

In 1983, Congress voted to establish a holiday to honor Martin Luther King Jr. The holiday was to be celebrated on the third Monday of January, just after Dr. King's birthday. The first official Martin Luther King Jr. Day was celebrated in January 1986.

⭐ On Martin Luther King Jr. Day, people take part in special events to honor King's work. Liberty City Parade in Miami, Florida, is one such event. For decades, thousands have attended the parade, which includes floats and bands.

Martin Luther King Jr. Day is a time to celebrate equality and freedom. On this special holiday, schools, banks, and offices are closed. Americans across the country remember Dr. King by honoring his teachings.

Today, Martin Luther King Jr. Day is celebrated in many ways. Thousands of people march in parades to show they are grateful for Dr. King's efforts. They also march to show support for the peaceful way he solved problems.

Independence Around the World

INDIA

October 2 is the anniversary of Mahatma Gandhi's birthday. This national holiday celebrates the life and work of Gandhi. He helped India become independent from Great Britain through nonviolent protest.

WORLDWIDE

Nelson Mandela was the first black president of South Africa. He wanted equality for all people. In 2009, the United Nations named Mandela's birthday an official day of action. It is called Nelson Mandela International Day.

WORLDWIDE

Human Rights Day is celebrated each year on December 10. This is the anniversary of the signing of the Universal Declaration of Human Rights. The declaration explains the rights of all humans.

Holiday Celebrations

This holiday is a time to think about tolerance and freedom. To celebrate, some people attend special church services. Others go to **conferences** and listen to social leaders talk about peace and civil rights.

✶✶ Today, many African Americans volunteer to work with young people in an effort to promote the arts and an appreciation for cultural diversity. The RALD Institute in Chicago is one such group.

In 2008, one year before being elected as the first African American president, Barack Obama, gave a speech on Martin Luther King Jr. Day at Dr. King's old church, the Ebenezer Baptist Church.

Many Americans spend Martin Luther King Jr. Day volunteering their time to help others. Dr. King believed that helping others was one of the best ways to overcome injustice. People all over the country honor Dr. King by serving their communities. They spend time with the elderly, cook food for the less fortunate, or tutor those who need help. Throughout the United States, Martin Luther King Jr. Day is a day of action.

After his death, Dr. King's widow Coretta Scott King, established the King Center in 1968, in Atlanta, Georgia. The King Center is part of the Martin Luther King Jr. National Historic Site. It is a place to learn more about Martin Luther King Jr. and the civil rights movement.

★ On January 13, 1979, the United States Postal Service issued a stamp in honor of Martin Luther King Jr.

Martin Luther King Jr. Day in the United States

People all over the United States observe Martin Luther King Jr. Day with special ceremonies. Here are just a few of the events that take place every year.

CALIFORNIA The Kingdom Day Parade takes place each year in Los Angeles. The parade is two miles long, and includes dance teams, marching bands, and more than 180 floats. After the parade, people gather for food and a concert.

California

Arizona

GEORGIA Many events take place in Atlanta, Georgia, Dr. King's hometown. People gather to listen to speeches during the three-day Martin Luther King Jr. Service Summit. They enjoy music, films, and a bus tour of Atlanta's civil rights landmarks. On the last day of the summit, everyone volunteers in the community.

ARIZONA In Mesa, Arizona, hundreds of people gather for the Mesa Martin Luther King Celebration and Parade. The parade features marching bands and school groups. The Mesa Martin Luther King Festival begins right after the parade. The festival offers musical entertainment and children's activities.

Hawai'i

0   970 Miles

Alaska

0   1,278 Miles

NEW YORK In New York City, New York, thousands join the Annual Martin Luther King Jr. Parade. People walk together for 25 blocks to celebrate Dr. King's life.

PENNSYLVANIA In Philadelphia, Pennsylvania, hundreds of people join in the Martin Luther King Jr. Day of Service. They honor Dr. King by volunteering at schools. Volunteers help by painting and cleaning the schools, or by mowing the schoolyard lawns.

New York

Pennsylvania

North Carolina

NORTH CAROLINA Many people in Raleigh, North Carolina, attend the Martin Luther King Wreath Laying Ceremony. Flowered wreaths are placed beside a statue of Dr. King to honor him.

BIRMINGHAM In Birmingham, Alabama, large crowds attend a special concert put on by the Alabama Symphony Orchestra. People from all over the city come to hear the musical tribute to Dr. King.

Alabama

Georgia

N
W — E
S

0   207 Miles

Holiday Symbols

Martin Luther King Jr. made a difference in peoples' lives. He helped improve society. As a result, Dr. King is honored throughout the United States. In some cities and towns, there have been special statues and monuments put up in Dr. King's memory. Other cities have dedicated parks to Dr. King, or named streets or buildings after him.

EBENEZER BAPTIST CHURCH

Martin Luther King Jr. was baptized at Ebenezer Baptist Church when he was 5 years old. He gave his first sermon to the **congregation** there when he was 17. In 1960, he became co-pastor of the church, sharing the duties with his father. After Dr. King was killed, hundreds of people gathered at Ebenezer Baptist Church for his funeral. Thousands more stood outside the church to pay their respects. Today, visitors can take tours of the historic church.

Jackson St NE 50

PARADES

Many cities and communities across the United States have parades to celebrate and honor Dr. King. They symbolize the many marches Dr. King led in the civil rights movement.

GRAVEYARD

Martin Luther King Jr.'s tomb is at the King Center. Every year, thousands of people visit his tomb. They sing songs, say prayers, and place flowers on the tomb. The visitors also read the important words inscribed on the tomb: "Free at last. Free at last. Thank God Almighty, I'm free at last." Dr. King spoke these words as part of his "I Have a Dream" speech.

A Speech to Remember

On August 28, 1963, Martin Luther King Jr. gave one of the best-known speeches in history. His "I Have a Dream" speech was greeted with thunderous applause by the crowd of more than 250,000 people standing along the National Mall in Washington, D.C.

"I say to you today, my friends, so even though we face the difficulties of today and tomorrow, I still have a dream. It is a dream deeply rooted in the American dream. I have a dream that one day this nation will rise up and live out the true meaning of its creed: "We hold these truths to be self-evident: that all men are created equal." I have a dream that my four little children will one day live in a nation where they will not be judged by the color of their skin but by the content of their character."

Martin Luther King Jr.

Write Your Own Speech

Leaders, such as Martin Luther King Jr., often give important speeches to express their views. Imagine you are the leader of a group or organization. Try writing a speech about something that you would like to improve about the world.

Think about the people who will be listening to your speech. What are their ages, cultural backgrounds, interests, and careers? Choose a topic that will be of interest to this group of people.

Think of a person or cause that you would like to support or something you would like to change to improve the world.

Brainstorm ideas for your speech. Write a concept web outlining some of the words you would like to say. Then, write your ideas as complete sentences. Be sure to use language that will entice your audience to listen.

Making an "I Have a Dream" Mobile

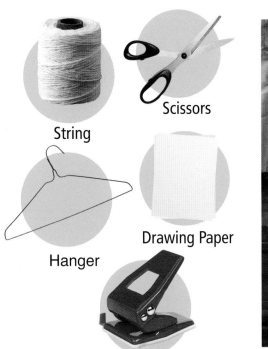

String

Scissors

Hanger

Drawing Paper

Hole punch

4 Easy Steps to Complete Your "I Have a Dream" Mobile

1 Cut out five clouds from the drawing paper.

2 On each cloud, draw a picture showing a dream that you have for your family, school, community, country, or the world.

3 Write a sentence about how you can help make your dream come true on the back of each cloud.

4 Hole-punch the top of the clouds. Tie one end of a string to each cloud. Tie the other end of the string to the hanger. Now, you have a dream mobile.

Making Church Social Biscuits

Here is an easy Martin Luther King Jr. Day treat to make. Adult supervision will be needed for this recipe.

What You Need

- 1 package active dry yeast
- 1/2 cup warm water
- 1/2 cup butter
- 1 egg
- 1/4 cup sugar
- 3 cups all–purpose flour
- 1 teaspoon salt
- 1/2 cup boiling water
- egg beater
- cookie sheet
- knife
- rolling pin
- large bowl

Directions

1. Melt the yeast in the warm water.
2. Beat together the butter, eggs, and sugar in the large bowl. Add the melted yeast, and stir.
3. Add flour, salt, and boiling water to the mixture, and mix well.
4. Refrigerate the dough overnight or until it is well chilled.
5. Roll out the dough to a 3/4 inch thickness, and cut it into biscuits.
6. Put the biscuits on the cookie sheet, and let them rise for about 1.5 to 2 hours.
7. Preheat the oven to 350º Fahrenheit.
8. Place the cookie sheet inside the oven, and cook until golden brown. This takes about 12 to 15 minutes.
9. You now have delicious church social biscuits to share with friends.

Yummy!

Test Your Knowledge!

1 On what date was Martin Luther King Jr. born?

2 What did Dr. King do for a living?

3 What well-known speech did Dr. King deliver in 1963?

4 What prize did Martin Luther King Jr. win in 1964?

5 On what date was Martin Luther King Jr. killed?

Quiz Answers:
1. Martin Luther King Jr. was born on January 15, 1929.
2. Martin Luther King Jr. was a minister in the Baptist church.
3. "I Have a Dream" is the name of the well-known speech Martin Luther King Jr. delivered in 1963.
4. In 1964, Martin Luther King Jr. won the Nobel Peace Prize.
5. Martin Luther King Jr. was killed on April 4, 1968.

Glossary

civil rights: rights of freedom and the pursuit of happiness, belonging to each person

civil rights movement: the political and social struggle for racial equality for African Americans

conferences: meetings

congregation: a group that gathers for religious worship

discrimination: treating people unfairly because of their skin color, race, or religion

equality: having equal rights for all people

injustice: a wrong act

protest: organized complaints

restricted: limited or prevented

segregation: forced separation

strike: to stop work

theology: the study of religion and the nature of God

unjust laws: rules that do not protect everyone's rights equally

Index

Log on to www.av2books.com

AV² by Weigl brings you media enhanced books that support active learning. Go to **www.av2books.com**, and enter the special code inside the front cover of this book. You will gain access to enriched and enhanced content that supplements and complements this book. Content includes video, audio, web links, quizzes, a slide show, and activities.

Audio
Listen to sections of the book read aloud.

Video
Watch informative video clips.

Web Link
Find research sites and play interactive games.

Try This!
Complete activities and hands-on experiments.

WHAT'S ONLINE?

Try This! Complete activities and hands-on experiments.	Web Link Find research sites and play interactive games.	Video Watch informative video clips.	EXTRA FEATURES
Pages 8-9 Write a biography about an important person	**Pages 6-7** Find out more about the history of Martin Luther King Jr. Day	**Pages 4-5** Watch a video about Martin Luther King Jr.	**Audio** Hear introductory audio at the top of every page
Pages 10-11 Describe the features and special events of a similar celebration around the world	**Pages 10-11** Learn more about similar celebrations around the world	**Pages 12-13** Check out a video about how people celebrate Martin Luther King Jr. Day	
Pages 14-15 Complete a mapping activity about Martin Luther King Jr. Day celebrations	**Pages 16-17** Find information about important holiday symbols		**Key Words** Study vocabulary, and play a matching word game.
Pages 16-17 Try this activity about important holiday symbols	**Pages 18-19** Link to more information about Martin Luther King Jr.		**Slide Show** View images and captions, and try a writing activity.
Pages 20-21 Play an interactive activity	**Pages 20-21** Check out more holiday craft ideas		**AV² Quiz** Take this quiz to test your knowledge

Due to the dynamic nature of the Internet, some of the URLs and activities provided as part of AV² by Weigl may have changed or ceased to exist. AV² by Weigl accepts no responsibility for any such changes. All media enhanced books are regularly monitored to update addresses and sites in a timely manner. Contact AV² by Weigl at 1-866-649-3445 or av2books@weigl.com with any questions, comments, or feedback.